Our Great Big World

DONNA HENDERSON

WestBow Press books may be ordered through booksellers or by contacting:

WestBow Press
A Division of Thomas Nelson & Zondervan
1663 Liberty Drive
Bloomington, IN 47403
www.westbowpress.com
844-714-3454

Interior Image Credit:
Alexa Alberto -Graphic Artist
Denise Fink - Art Contributor

ISBN: 978-1-6642-6091-7 (sc)
ISBN: 978-1-6642-6092-4 (e)

Library of Congress Control Number: 2022904989

Print information available on the last page.

WestBow Press rev. date: 03/31/2022

WESTBOW
PRESS®
A DIVISION OF THOMAS NELSON
& ZONDERVAN

God loved us so much.
He made a great big
world and called it
Earth.
For six days, God made
wonderful things to put
on the earth that would
make us happy.

The Story of Our Great Big World

4

Day 1

On the first day, the world was very dark.
God said the earth needed light.
He made beautiful light
and called it the day,
the dark He called the night.

God liked what He made
and said it was good.

6

Day 2

On the second day,
God made lots of water.
He also made a beautiful sky.

God liked what He made
and said it was good.

8

Day 3

On the third day, God
made dry land.
He made water to go
around the dry land,
He called the water *sea*.
God also made many plants,
trees, seeds, and fruit
for this beautiful earth.

God liked what He made
and said it was good.

Day 4

On the fourth day,
God made the warm sun
and called it *daytime*.
He made the moon and
called it *nighttime*.
He made the twinkling stars
in the sky for us to
enjoy at night.

God liked what He made
and said it was good.

12

Day 5

On the fifth day, God made great
swimming creatures and
fish in the sea.
He made beautiful birds
that fly in the sky.

God liked what He made
and said it was good.

Day 6

On the sixth day, God made cows;
creeping, crawling creatures;
bugs; and animals.
God wanted someone to take care
of all these things, so
he made a man named Adam.
God did not want Adam to be lonely,
so later, He made Adam a wife
and called her Eve.

God liked what He made
and said it was good.

16

Day 7

On the seventh day, God looked
at what He had made.
He said all these things were good
and made a day to rest.
God made this great big world for us.
He wants us to enjoy it and take care of it.

Why don't you bow your head, close your eyes, and
thank God for all He made for us.

On day 1, God made light and dark. Can you find the light and dark?

On day 2, God made the clouds in the sky. Can you find the clouds in the sky?

On day 3, God made trees. Can you find a tree?

On day 4, God made sun for the daytime. Can you find the sun?

On day 5 God created fish. Can you find fish?

On day 6, God made Adam. Can you find Adam?

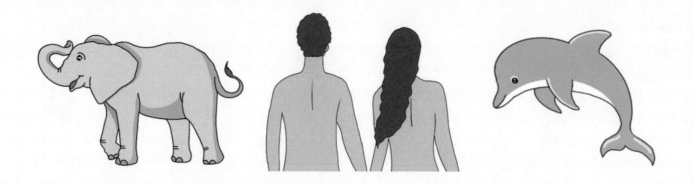

Draw something God made for us.

Printed in the United States
by Baker & Taylor Publisher Services